Astronomy

Graham Peacock and Dennis Ashton

Thomson Learning • New York

Books in the series:

ASTRONOMY • ELECTRICITY • FORCES
GEOLOGY • HEAT • LIGHT • MATERIALS
METEOROLOGY • SOUND • WATER

First published in the
United States in 1994 by
Thomson Learning
115 Fifth Avenue
New York, NY 10003

First published in Great Britain in 1994 by
Wayland (Publishers) Ltd.

UK version copyright © 1994 Wayland (Publishers) Ltd.

U.S. version copyright © 1994 Thomson Learning

Library of Congress Cataloging-in-Publication Data
Peacock, Graham.
 Astronomy / Graham Peacock and Dennis Ashton.
   p.   cm. – (Science activities)
 Includes bibliographical references and index.
 ISBN: 1-56847-191-2
 1. Astronomy – Juvenile literature. 2. Astronomy
 – Experiments – Juvenile literature. [1. Astronomy.]
 I. Ashton, Dennis. II. Title. III. Series.
 QB46.P43   1994
 520 – dc20   94-16933

Printed in Italy

Acknowledgments
The publishers would like to thank the following for allowing their pictures to be used in this book: Bryan & Cherry Alexander 11; Chapel Studios 5; Image Select 20 (bottom left); Paul Crowder & Steve Ibbotson 23 (top right), 24 (left & right), 27 (bottom left); Science Photo Library *cover* (center & bottom right), 7, 13, 14, 20 (bottom right), 23 (bottom right), 25, 27 (top right), 28. All commissioned photographs are from the Wayland Picture Library (Zul Mukhida). All artwork is by Tony de Saulles.

Contents

The turning Earth	4
Day and night	6
Seasons	8
Seasonal changes	10
The sky in daylight	12
The sky at night	13
The moon's surface	14
Phases of the moon	16
Planet models	18
Observing planets	20
Constellations	22
Observing the night sky: March–August	24
Observing the night sky: September–February	26
Meteors	28
Glossary	30
Books to read	31
Chapter notes	31
Index	32

Words that appear in **bold** are explained in the glossary on page 30.

The turning Earth

Our **planet** Earth moves in space in different ways. It turns or spins on its **axis** once every 24 hours; this gives us day and night. Earth's axis is tilted, and that tilt, together with the Earth's **orbiting** the sun, gives us the **seasons**. Eight other planets orbit the sun, but it seems that the Earth is the only one on which there is life. The sun is a star, one of the millions in the universe. In this book you will explore the night sky and discover some of the many wonders it contains, and Earth's place in the universe. This is the study of astronomy.

How do sundials work?

You will need:
- a sunny place outside ◆ a thin pole or stick
- a large sheet of paper ◆ a felt-tip pen
- a plastic cup ◆ 4 weights

1. In a sunny place, push the pole into the ground. (If the ground is too hard, push the pole into a container of sand or soil.)

2. Rest the plastic cup upside down on top of the pole to protect your eyes.

3. Put weights on the corners of the paper. Place the paper on the ground next to the pole.

4. Draw around the shadow position on the paper once each hour, and write down the time beside it.

If you were to look down at the North **Pole** from space, you would see Earth rotating counterclockwise. From Earth, this rotation makes it look as if the sun moves from east to west across the sky.

Make a shadowmeter

You will need:
- a sunny place ◆ a ruler
- a pencil ◆ a sheet of 8½-by-11-inch paper

1. Using the measurements shown in the diagram below, draw nine lines across the sheet of paper.

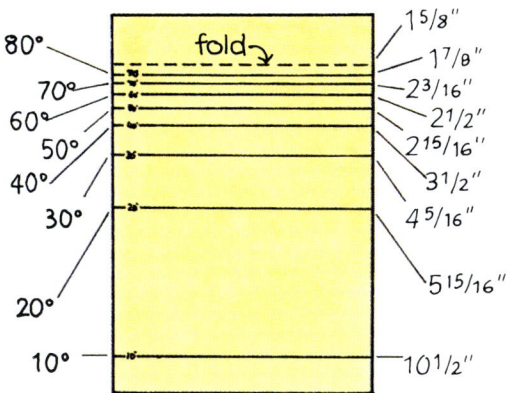

2. Label the lines with the angles.

3. Make a crease along the first 1⅝ inch line and fold the paper up at an angle of 90°.

4. Put the shadowmeter on a table in the sunlight so that the folded end makes a shadow on the paper behind.

5. Record the angle made by the sun's shadow at different times of the day.

Garden sundials cast a shadow on a flat plate that has hour lines marked on it.

Sun time

Use your sundial or shadowmeter to tell the time on the next sunny day. Check your results with a watch or clock.

Day and night

Why do we have day and night?

You will need:
- a globe on a stand
- a strong light
- a piece of clay

1. Find the region where you live on the globe. Mark it with a piece of clay.

2. Shine the light on the globe level with the **equator**.

3. Look at the globe and turn it slowly counterclockwise.

Which states come into the light at the same time as your own?

Which countries are getting dark when your region is just getting light?

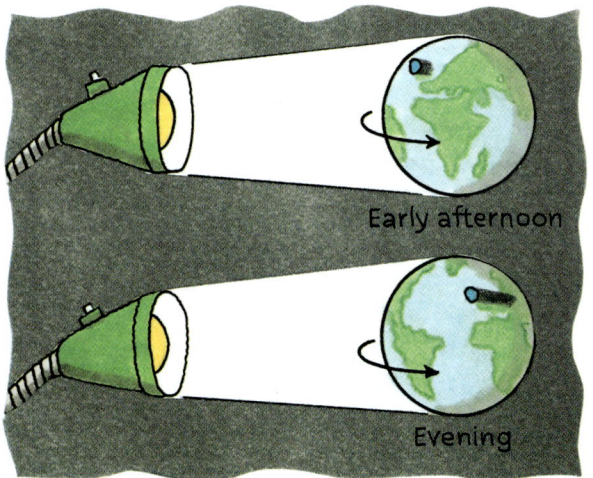

Look at the direction of the shadow made by the clay. It changes at different times of day. The shadow moves like that of the shadowmeter.

Find out:

Look at the globe. Which country would you reach if you could dig through the middle of the earth?

Use your globe and light to find out if it is morning, afternoon, or night there now.

Seasonal day length

You will need:

◆ a notebook and pencil ◆ a magnetic compass

1. At sunset, use the compass to find west.
2. In your notebook, sketch the buildings and landmarks that you see.
3. Show the place where the sun sets.
4. Write down the time and date.

December 20 3:35pm

5. Leave a space in your notebook to do this again at a different time of year.

August 18 8:10pm

Day length

Find the times of sunset and sunrise in the newspaper. What is the length of the day? Do this again one week later. Are the days getting shorter or longer?

Viewed from space, Earth is half in the light and half in darkness.

Seasons

Why do the seasons happen?

You will need:
- a globe on a stand
- a strong light

1. Shine the light on the globe, level with the equator. Turn the globe so that the northern part tilts away from the light. This is winter for the northern **hemisphere**.

2. Find the **Arctic Circle**. Slowly turn the globe counterclockwise. Notice that north of this line there is continuous night.

3. Move the globe so that the northern part tilts toward the light. This is summer for the northern hemisphere. Notice that north of the Arctic Circle there is continuous daylight.

The Earth's axis is tilted by about 23°. The effect of the tilt gives us different seasons. Most globes are set on their stands to show this tilt.

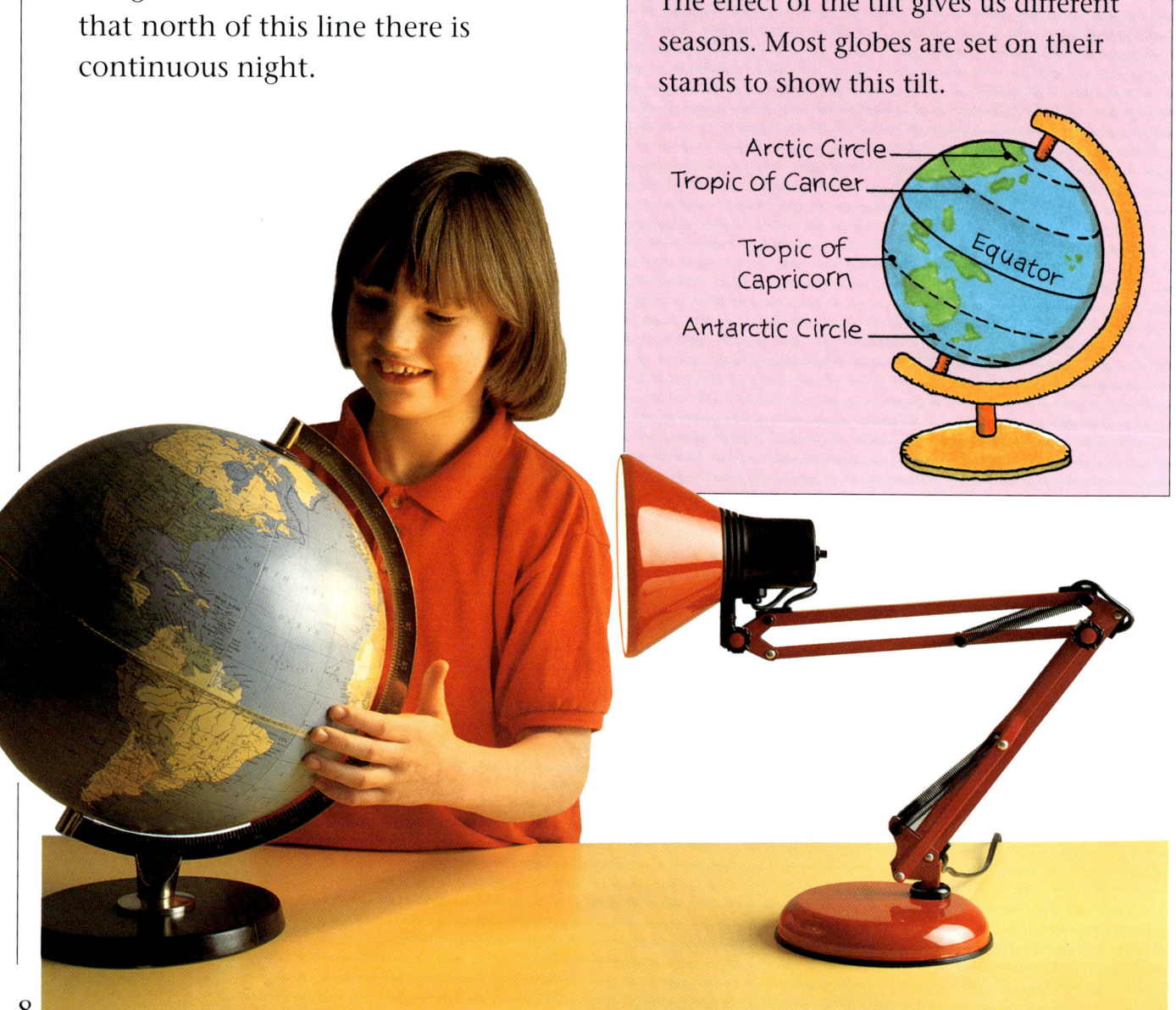

Why is it hotter in summer?

You will need:
◆ a flashlight with a narrow beam ◆ a globe

1. In a dark room, shine the flashlight straight at the equator. Look at the ring of light.

2. From the same place, shine the light at the North Pole. Notice how the beam of light spreads out. This means the heat is also spread out.

The same amount of heat is spread over a larger area. This is why it is always hotter near the equator.

3. Shine the flashlight on your region in its winter and summer positions. Notice that the beam is more spread out in winter.

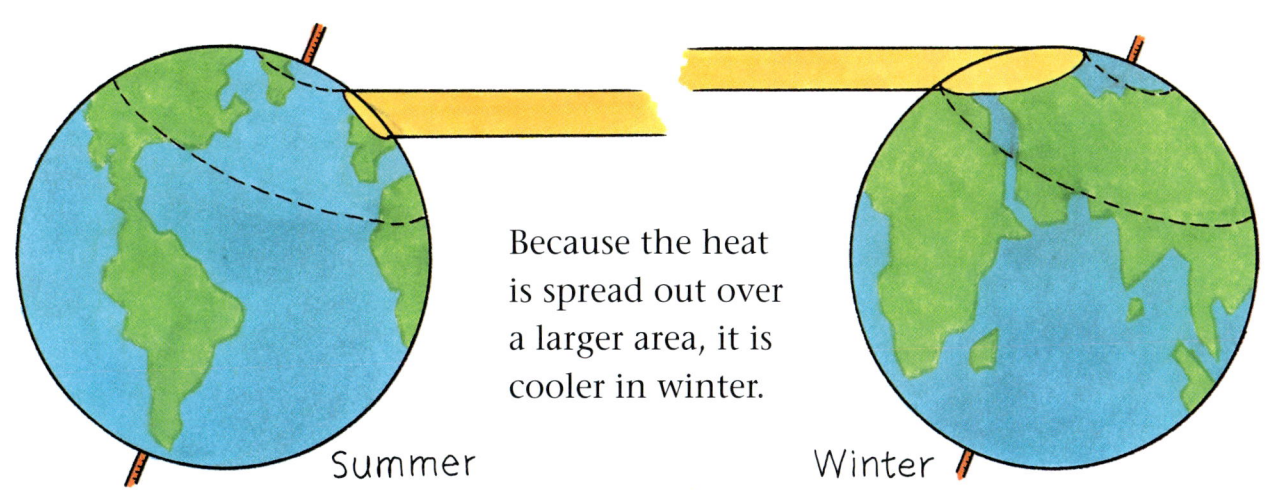

Because the heat is spread out over a larger area, it is cooler in winter.

Summer　　　Winter

Seasonal changes

Why are the days so short in winter?

You will need:
- a globe on a stand
- a strong light
- a piece of clay

1. Find your nearest city on the globe and mark it with a piece of clay. Position the globe so that it is winter in the city.

2. Shine the light on the globe and position it so that the clay is on the edge of the light. Find out how much daylight the city gets in winter by counting the number of **lines of longitude** that are in the light. (Count around the globe along the city's **line of latitude.**)

3. Now move the globe around so that it is summer in the city and repeat the exercise. Then compare the city's day length in winter and in summer.

4. Find a city a long way north or south of your city and on the same line of longitude.

5. Which place gets more daylight in winter? Which gets more daylight in summer?

Longitude and latitude

Lines of longitude and latitude are imaginary lines running around the Earth. Lines of longitude run between the north and south poles. Lines of latitude run parallel to the equator. Each line of longitude represents about 40 minutes of time.

Greenwich Meridian

The line of 0° longitude was fixed at Greenwich, England, in 1884. It was first set to make the same local time for railway trains. Before this, the time of noon could vary within a few miles across a country.

Did you know?

In some parts of the Arctic Circle there is continuous daylight for up to four months.

This is Moriusaq Village in the Arctic Circle. The sun in the Arctic Circle never sets for certain parts of the year.

Height of the Sun

You will need:
- a magnetic compass
- a notebook and pencil

1. Use a compass to find south.

2. Look south on a sunny day at 3 PM. Sketch the buildings and landmarks and draw the position of the sun. Write down the date and time under your sketch.

3. Leave the opposite page blank so that you can do the same at a different time of year.

What do you notice about the height of the sun in the two drawings?

3pm December 11

3pm June 2

Solstice

In the northern hemisphere the sun is at its highest on June 21. This is the summer solstice. It is at its lowest on December 21. This is the winter solstice.

Equinox

March 21 and September 23 are equinoxes. They are the only two days in the year when the sun is directly overhead at the equator. On these two dates, day and night are of equal length at every point on the globe.

The sky in daylight

How can you safely observe the sun?

You will need:

- a sunny place ◆ binoculars or a telescope ◆ a tripod
- a large piece of cardboard ◆ white paper ◆ scissors

Never look directly at the sun through binoculars or with the naked eye.

1. If you are using binoculars, cover the left eyepiece with a lens cover.

2. Fix the binoculars or telescope on the tripod. Point them in the general direction of the sun.

3. Cut a hole in the cardboard and fix it around the front of the binoculars or telescope to make some shadow.

4. Hold a piece of paper behind the eyepiece and move it until you see a bright circle of light on the paper.

5. Focus the circle using the focusing ring on the binoculars or telescope.

Can you see darker spots within the bright circle of light? These are sunspots.

Sunspots are cooler areas on the sun's surface.

If you were to watch the sunspots over a period of days, you would see them move across the sun's surface as it rotates.

The sky at night

What is a good way to look at the evening sky?

Binoculars are very handy to use for looking at the moon and stars. Their strength is shown by two numbers:

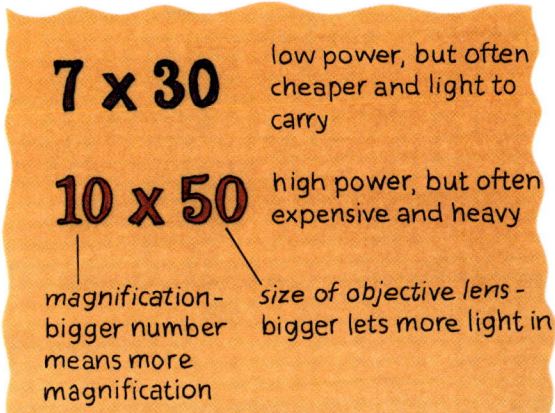

7 x 30 — low power, but often cheaper and light to carry

10 x 50 — high power, but often expensive and heavy

magnification - bigger number means more magnification

size of objective lens - bigger lets more light in

Large telescopes like this one are built in clear air at the top of mountains, far away from interference from city lights.

Find a place well away from street lights to observe the evening sky.

Adjust your eyes

You will need:
- a dark room with a light switch

1. Go into a darkened room.
2. Turn on the light for a minute or two.
3. Turn it off.
4. How long is it before you get used to the dark?

Light gets into your eye through your pupil. Your pupil changes size to adjust to different amounts of light. In a little light your pupil gets bigger. In lots of light your pupil is smaller. It takes time to adjust to seeing in the dark.

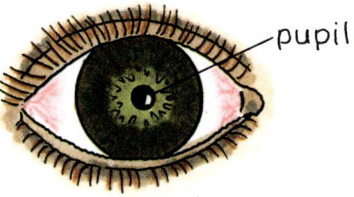

lots of light

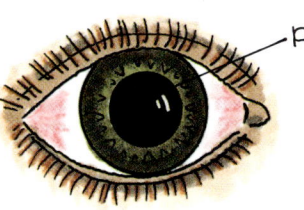

little light

Did you know?

Red light won't dazzle you at night. It won't spoil your night vision in the same way as white light.

Be safe

Always tell your parents where you are going and who you are going with.

Never go alone. It's safer and more fun with friends.

Be sure to wear warm clothes.

The moon's surface

You will need:
- a flashlight or lamp to write by
- binoculars
- a notebook and pencil

1. Study the moon through your binoculars.
2. Try to find the features shown here.
3. Do a drawing in your notebook. Label all the features you can see.

Ancient rocks

The oldest rocks on the moon are about 4.6 billion years old.

Features labeled on the moon: Sea of Serenity, Sea of Tranquility, Sea of Nectar, Hadley Rille (Rift Valley), Julius Caesar, Copernicus, Kepler, Tycho

Did you know?

The temperature on the sunny side of the moon can be over 220°F. In the shadow it is below −300°F.

Craters

These were formed by meteorites (pieces of rock) hitting the moon. Others were formed by long-extinct volcanoes.

Seas

The dark areas of the moon were once seas of molten lava. They were caused by huge flows of lava from volcanoes. Now they are solid plains of hardened lava.

How were the craters formed?

You will need:
- a small basin
- damp sand
- a small, heavy ball or stone

1. Put some sand in the basin.
2. Drop the ball or stone onto the sand.
3. Try throwing the ball or stone from close range.
4. Notice the shapes the ball or stone leaves in the sand.

Enormous craters

The deepest craters on the moon are more than five miles deep.

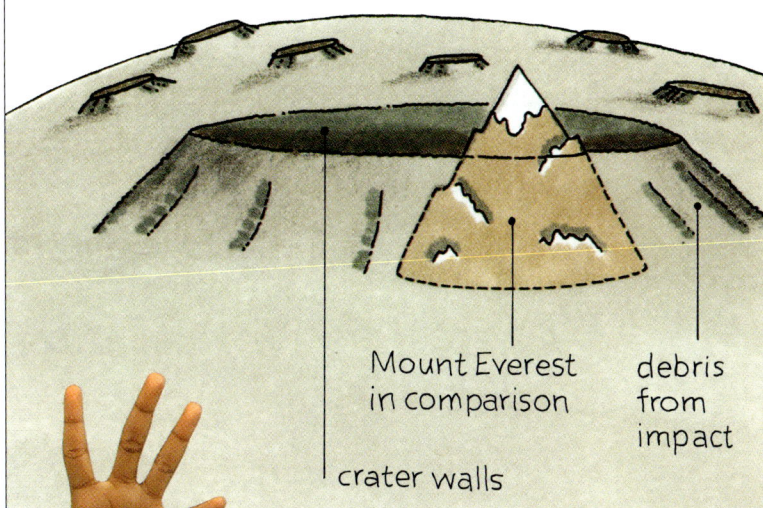

Mount Everest in comparison | debris from impact | crater walls

The moon's diameter is about the same as the width of Australia.

Craters are also found on the surfaces of the planets Mars and Venus. Scientists believe that these craters and those on the moon were formed at the same time the planets were, over four billion years ago.

The moon also has large mountain ranges rising to 33,000 feet above the surface.

Phases of the moon

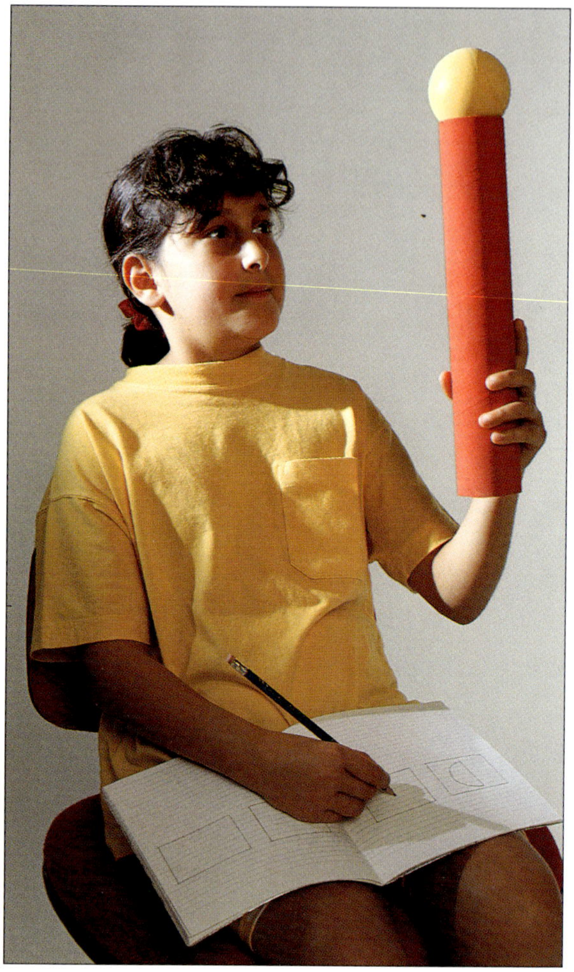

You will need:

- a small, light-colored ball, to represent the moon
- a straight beam of light, to represent the sun
- you, to represent Earth
- a cardboard tube to hold the ball
- a stool
- a notebook and pencil

1 In a dark room, sit on the stool and balance the ball on top of the tube.

2 Hold the ball up into the light. Draw the shape the light makes on the ball.

3 Turn yourself counterclockwise. Draw the new shape of the light on the ball.

4 Do this for at least four different positions.

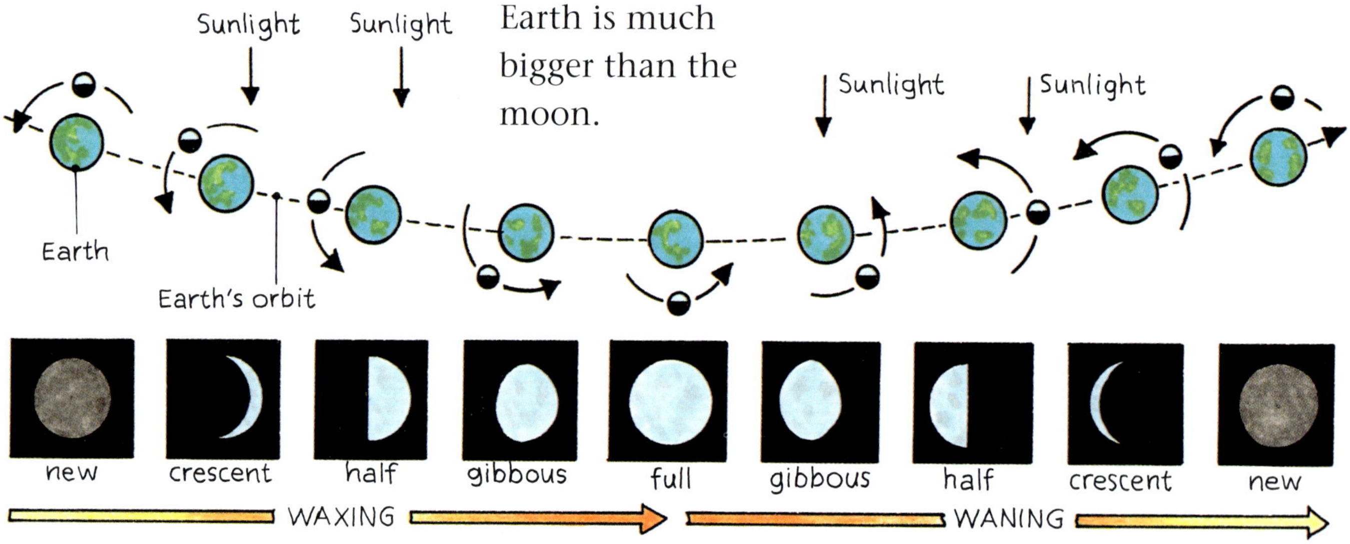

Sunlight
Sunlight
Earth is much bigger than the moon.
Sunlight
Sunlight
Earth
Earth's orbit
new
crescent
half
gibbous
full
gibbous
half
crescent
new
WAXING
WANING

The moon takes $29^1/_2$ days to go from new moon to the next new moon.

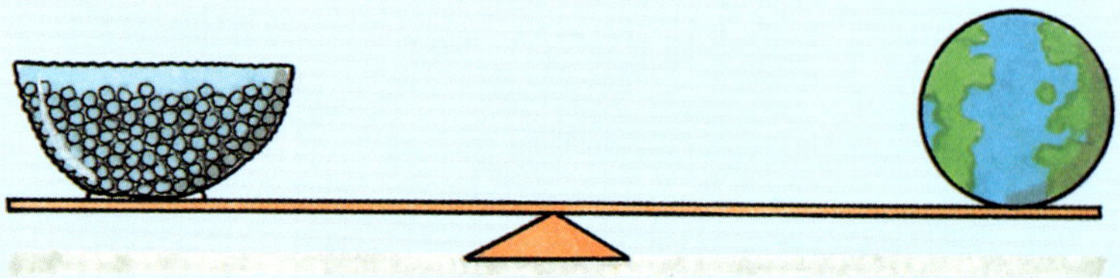

Earth weighs as much as eighty moons.

Make a moon chart

You will need:
- a notebook and pencil
- a ruler
- a large piece of paper

1. Draw thirty equal-size squares on a double page of your notebook.
2. Date each square starting with today.
3. Look for the moon every night for twenty nights.
4. If you see the moon, draw its shape in the correct square.
5. If the weather is cloudy, put in a cloud symbol.
6. Use the last ten squares to predict the shape of the moon for those days. Check to see if your predictions are correct.
7. With your friends, make a large moon chart, like the one in the photo, using the results from your moon watch.

Same face

The same side of the moon always faces the Earth. We only know about the other side of the moon because of the spacecraft that have orbited it.

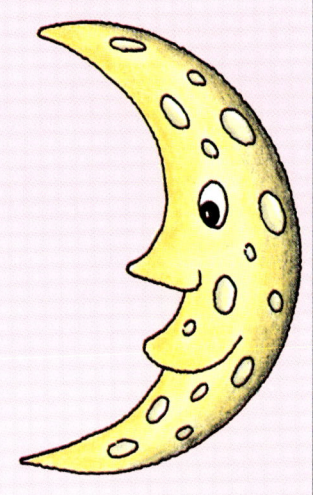

Moonrise and moonset

You will need:
- a magnetic compass
- a notebook and pencil

1. Use the compass to find east and west.
2. Look east for the place where the moon rises.
3. Look west for where it sets.
4. Record the times it rises and sets in your notebook.

The moon is 240,000 miles away from Earth. It **orbits** at $6/10$ of a mile per second.

Planet models

What do the planets look like?

You will need:
- a compass and a pencil
- a ruler
- different-colored paints
- some cardboard
- scissors

1. Set the compass for the radius shown in the table below. Draw circles for each planet.

2. Paint each planet according to the colors in the diagram.

Planet	Approx radius (mi.)	Radius of model
Mercury	1,500	1/2 inch
Venus	3,800	1 1/4 inches
Earth	3,900	1 1/4 inches
Mars	2,100	3/4 inch
Jupiter	45,000	15 inches
Saturn	38,000	12 1/2 inches
Uranus	16,000	5 1/2 inches
Neptune	16,000	5 1/2 inches
Pluto	1,000	1/3 inch

Scale

On this scale the sun would have to be a cardboard disk with a radius of 145 inches.

How far apart are the planets?

You will need:

◆ a piece of paper or wallpaper, 3 feet long ◆ a ruler ◆ tape ◆ scissors ◆ a felt-tip pen

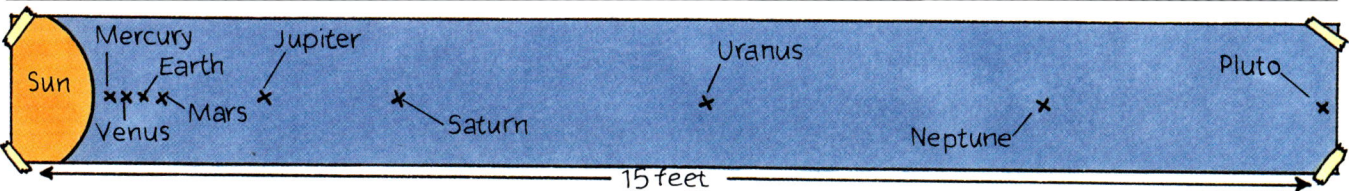

1. Fold the paper in five, lengthwise. Cut the paper into five lengths. Tape them together, end to end, so that you have a wall chart strip 15 feet long. Draw the sun at one end.

2. Use this table to mark the positions of the planets on your wall chart with crosses and labels.

Planet	Actual distance from sun (millions mi.)	Distance along the wall chart
Mercury	36.25	2/3 inch
Venus	67.5	1 1/8 inches
Earth	93.75	1 1/2 inches
Mars	142.5	2 1/3 inches
Jupiter	486.25	8 inches
Saturn	893.125	15 inches
Uranus	1,796.875	30 inches
Neptune	2,815	47 inches
Pluto	3,687.5	61 1/2 inches

Scale of wall chart is 1 inch = 60,000,000 miles.

Vacation among the stars

Write a travel brochure for your favorite planet.

Planet file

Make a set of cards or a computer database for the planets.

Add information to each card as you find it.

Observing planets

You can often see the planets Venus, Mars, Jupiter, or Saturn without binoculars. Planets are slightly bigger than the other stars. They are visible at different times of the year.

You can find out which planets are visible now by looking in today's newspaper or a current astronomy magazine and making a note of when and where to look for them in the sky.

Planet watch

You will need:

◆ binoculars or a telescope ◆ a notebook and pencil

Observing Venus

Venus follows the sun, so it is easiest to see just after sunset. Venus is often one of the brightest object in the sky.

1 Draw the position of Venus. Add the date and the time.

2 Use the binoculars to see Venus more clearly.

3 Record its shape in your book.

Observing Mars

Mars is called the red planet. Its soil contains iron oxide (rust), which makes it look slightly red.

1 In your notebook draw the position of Mars and nearby stars.

2 Repeat your observations and records each clear night.

3 Predict where Mars will be in a week's time.

4 Check to see if your prediction was correct.

Venus often has a crescent shape like the moon.

Observing Jupiter

Jupiter has four large moons visible through binoculars. The moons look like tiny stars in a line near the planet.

1. Draw Jupiter and its moons in your notebook.
2. Repeat the observations on other nights.
3. How do you think the moons are moving?

Write down your ideas.

Observing Saturn

1. In your notebook draw Saturn and any nearby stars.
2. If you have one, use a telescope to look at Saturn and its rings.
3. Draw a picture of your observation in your notebook.

You will need a telescope if you want to see the rings of Saturn.

Did you know?

Saturn's rings are made of chunks of ice and rock that are in orbit around the planet. They may be fragments of a moon pulled apart by Saturn's **gravity**.

Venus and Mars are small, rocky planets like Earth. Jupiter and Saturn are giant planets made of gas.

Saturn is so light that it would float on water—if you could find a big enough bucket!

Constellations

Constellations are patterns of stars in the night sky. They are like dot-to-dot pictures that make shapes of animals and objects. There are eighty-eight constellations in the sky.

Shoebox constellations

You will need:
- a shoebox ◆ a straight pin
- scissors ◆ tape ◆ a pencil
- tracing paper ◆ a picture of a constellation (e.g., the Big Dipper on page 23)

1. Place the tracing paper on the constellation picture.

2. Draw pencil dots on the main stars.

3. Place the tracing paper over the end of the shoebox.

4. Use the pin to make holes through the dots and the end of the box.

5. Cut a small viewing hole about $1/2$ inch across at the opposite end of the box.

6. Fix the box lid on with tape.

7. Hold your constellation box up to a light and look through the viewing hole to see the constellation of stars.

Looking for the Big Dipper and Polaris (northern hemisphere only)

You will need:
- a clear, dark sky
- a notebook and pencil
- a flashlight
- a magnetic compass

1. Use your compass to find north.

2. In the north, find the seven stars that make a shape like a saucepan with a bent handle. This is called the Big Dipper.

3. Follow the end two stars of the saucepan to Polaris, the North Star.

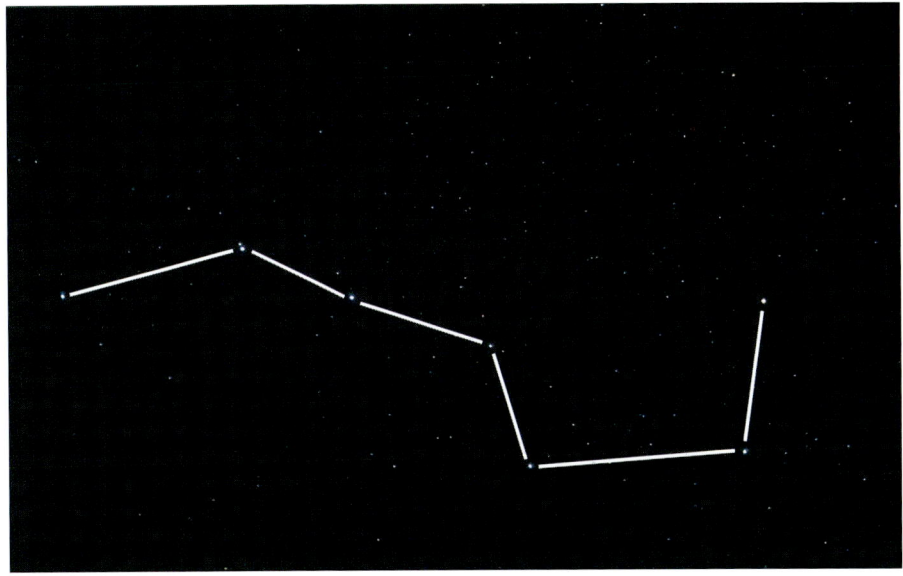

This photo shows the Big Dipper constellation. You cannot see Polaris in this photo, but the diagram below shows you how to find it. The Big Dipper is actually part of a larger constellation, Ursa Major.

Did you know?

Polais is almost directly above Earth's North Pole. It is the only star that stays in the same place as our Earth turns on its axis.

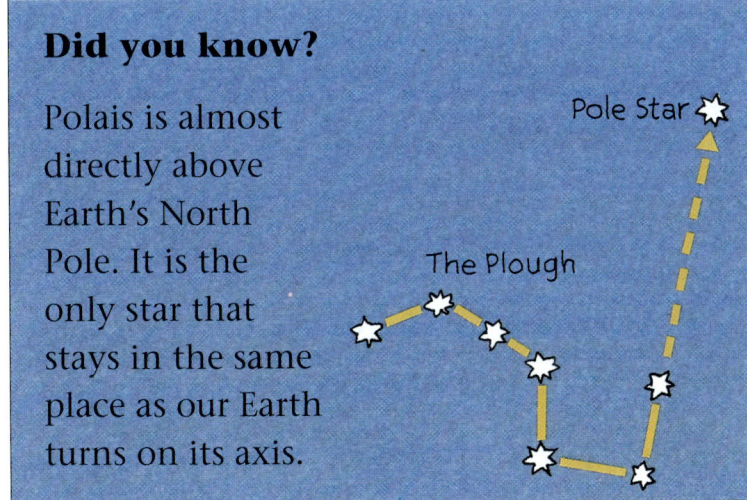

The Southern Cross is a diamond-shaped constellation that you can only see in the southern hemisphere.

Southern hemisphere

In the southern hemisphere, the sky is different from the north. You can see most of the constellations at the same time as you would see them in the north. However they appear in different positions, often upside-down compared to the northern sky.

Observing the night sky

The sky in March, April, and May

As Earth orbits the sun, we see different stars at different times of year.

You will need:
- a flashlight
- a notebook and pencil
- binoculars or a telescope
- a magnetic compass

Remember that if you live in the southern hemisphere, the constellations may look different from those in the pictures here. However, you can find all of them by looking north instead of south.

Leo the Lion

1 Find the stars of Leo in the south. (Look for the big backward question mark).

2 Draw the stars of Leo in your notebook.

3 Sketch the shape of a lion around the stars.

4 Find Regulus, the bright star at the bottom of the question mark.

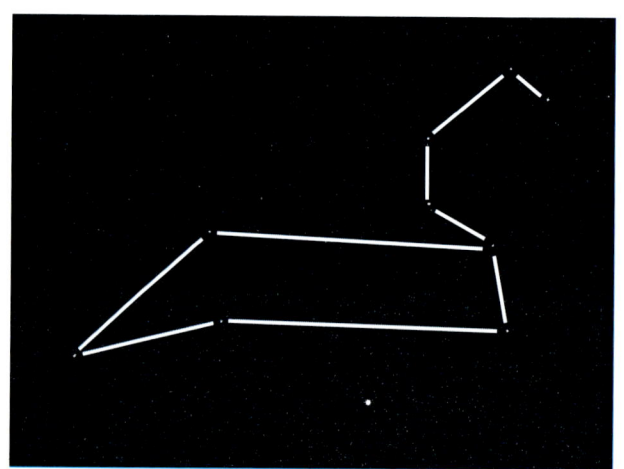

Boötes the Herdsman

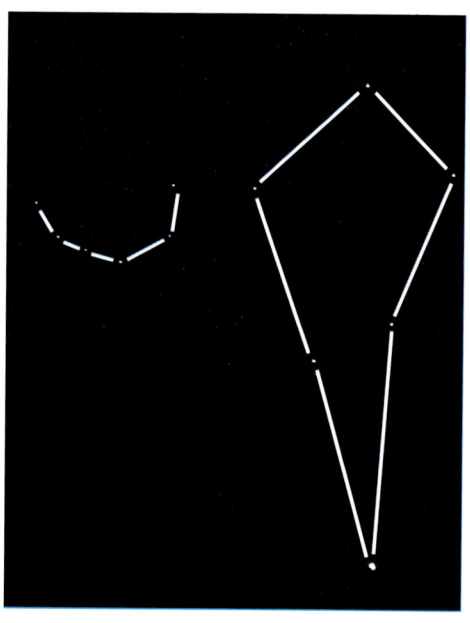

1 Find the Big Dipper almost overhead.

2 Follow the handle of the Big Dipper down to a bright orange star called Arcturus.

3 Look above Arcturus for stars in the shape of a kite. This is Boötes. (In the southern hemisphere you can spot Boötes by looking north in March for the shape of a kite.)

4 Near the top left of the kite is a curve of six stars. It is the Northern Crown, or Corona Borealis.

5 Draw Boötes and the Crown in your notebook.

6 Look at Regulus and Arcturus with binoculars. Record their colors in your notebook.

The sky in June, July, and August

Triangulum, the Triangle

1. Look south for three bright stars making a huge triangle. These are Deneb (top), Vega (right), and Altair (bottom).

2. Look at the three stars through binoculars. Record their colors in your notebook.

3. Look below Deneb for three stars which, together with Deneb, make a cross. This is Cygnus, the Swan.

4. In your notebook, make your own drawing of the stars in the Triangle. Label the stars and constellations.

5. Use binoculars to look at Cygnus. You will see thousands of stars. This is part of the band of stars that make up our **galaxy**, called the **Milky Way**.

> **Did you know?**
>
> The colors of stars depend on their temperatures. The hottest stars are blue; the least hot are red.

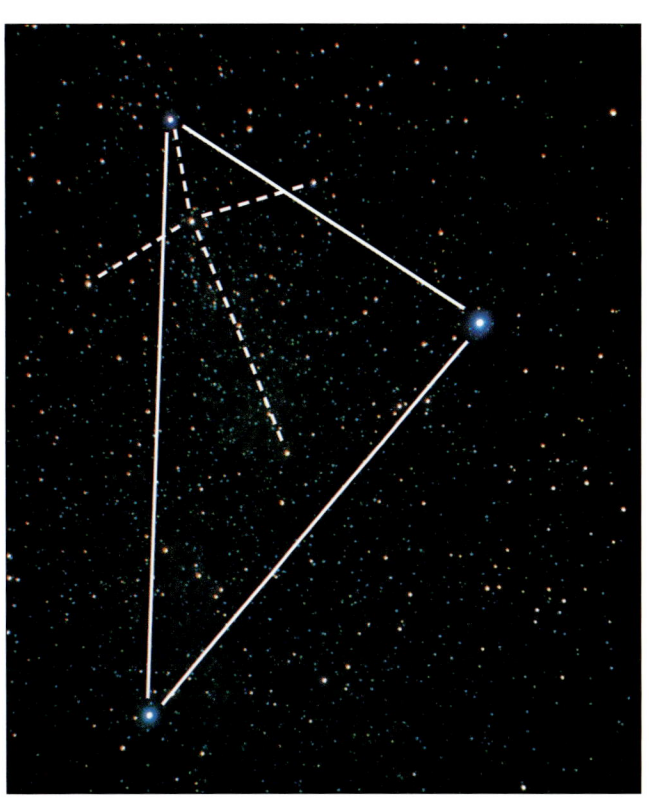

> **Did you know?**
>
> Our galaxy is like a giant Frisbee. When we look into our galaxy we see a band of stars stretching across the sky. This is the Milky Way.

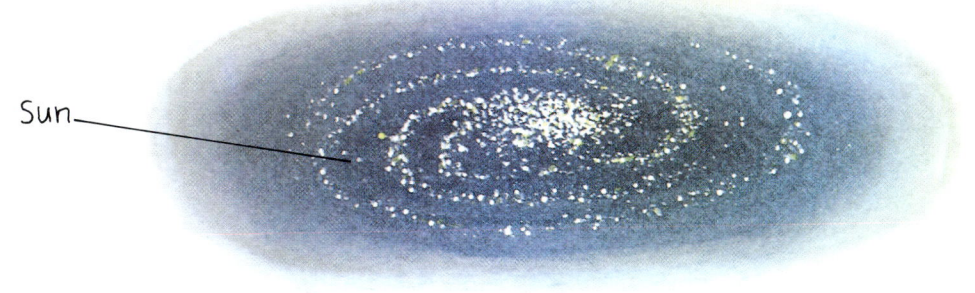

Observing the night sky

The sky in September, October, and November

Pegasus and Andromeda

1 Look south for four stars making the huge square of Pegasus.

2 Draw the stars of Pegasus in your book.

3 Join the stars to show Pegasus as the flying horse. (He is upside down.)

4 Look for a line of stars running from the top left of the square. This is Andromeda, the princess.

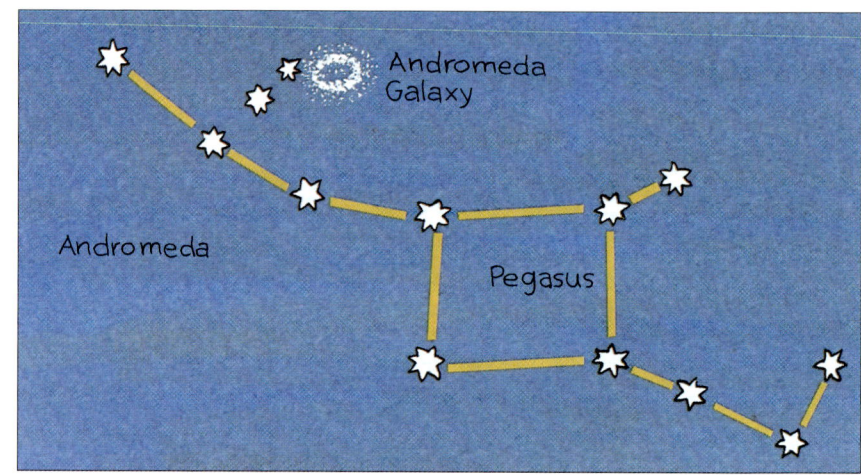

5 Look carefully above Andromeda's second star. You will see a faint, fuzzy glow—this is the great galaxy Andromeda.

Andromeda is named after a character from ancient Greek mythology. Andromeda was the daughter of Queen Cassiopeia. When a sea monster threatened the coast of their country, Andromeda was chosen as a sacrifice. She was rescued just in time by Perseus.

Did you know?

The Andromeda galaxy is the closest spiral galaxy to our own Milky Way. Even so, its light takes over two million years to reach us.

The sky in December, January, and February

Orion the Hunter

1 Look in the south for the stars of Orion. You can find them from the three stars in a line which make the hunter's belt.

2 Draw the stars in your book. Label the stars Betelgeuse (top left) and Rigel (bottom right).

3 Note the colors of Betelgeuse and Rigel.

4 Look below the three stars in the belt —imagine a sword hanging down. You will see a hazy patch of light. This is the Orion nebula, a huge cloud of glowing gas.

5 Look at the nebula through binoculars or a telescope.

Did you know?

Betelgeuse is a red supergiant star. If it replaced the sun, it would stretch out beyond the orbit of Mars.

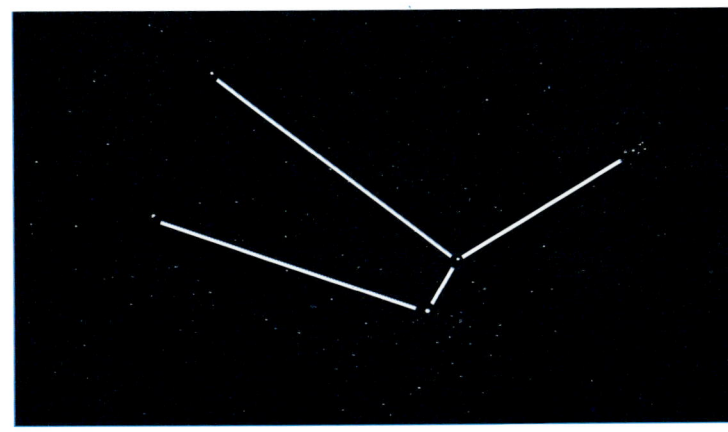

Taurus the Bull

1 Follow the belt of Orion upward to a bright orange star. This is Aldebaran, the eye of Taurus the Bull.

2 Find two bright stars above and to the left of Aldebaran. These are the bull's horns. (See left.)

3 Look above and to the right of Aldebaran for a twinkling patch of stars. This is the Pleiades star cluster, or Seven Sisters.

4 Look at the Pleiades cluster through binoculars. See if you can count the stars in the cluster.

Meteors

Fragments of rock and dust traveling through space are called **meteors**. When meteors enter Earth's atmosphere, they are traveling at enormous speed. Friction makes the material burn up, leaving a streak of light that people call "shooting stars." Meteors often fall in numbers. This is called a meteor shower.

When to look for meteors

Look at the meteor shower table below and plan a good night for a meteor watch with your friends.

A meteor, or "shooting star," plunging through space, leaving a fiery trail.

Name of Meteor Shower	Best time to look for them	Maximum number per hour
Quadrantids	January 4th	100
Lyrids	April 21st-23rd	10
Aquarids	May 4th-6th	20
Aquarids	July 27th	30
Perseids	August 9th-14th	70
Orionids	October 19th-21st	30
Taurids	November 7th	10
Geminids	December 10th-15th	60

Did you know?

Meteor showers come from pieces of rock and dust left by old comets.

Recording a meteor shower

You will need:
- a clear, dark sky
- a comfortable chair
- a large piece of paper
- a flashlight or lamp
- colored pencils
- a magnetic compass

1 Use your compass to find east and sit facing that direction.

2 Draw an outline of the horizon in the east. Add in the bright stars that you see.

3 When you see a meteor, draw its track on your diagram, using an arrow to show the length and direction.

4 Beside the arrow write down the meteor's:

- brightness (bright, medium, or dim)
- color
- whether it left a "train" (a glow behind it)
- unusual features e.g., explosions along its path

What do you notice about your meteor tracks?

Meteor showers come from the same point in the sky. This point is called the meteor radiant.

East

True or false?

1. Earth rotates counterclockwise.
2. The line of 0° longitude passes through Greenwich, Connecticut.
3. You could swim in the Sea of Tranquility.
4. We always see the same face of the moon.
5. The biggest planet is Neptune.
6. Polaris is another name for the North Star.
7. Saturn is the only planet with rings.
8. It takes over two million years for light to reach us from the Andromeda galaxy.

The answers are on page 32.

Glossary

Arctic Circle The line of 70° (N) latitude on the globe. On and to the north of this line on June 21 there is continuous daylight.

Axis A line about which a rotating body turns. Earth spins around its axis once a day, tilted at an angle of 23°.

Binoculars A form of double telescope with an eyepiece for each eye.

Constellations Groups of stars appearing in the same part of the sky.

Equator The line around a ball at right angles to the axis.

Galaxy A huge collection of stars separated by enormous distances. Galaxies contain billions of stars, and there are billions of galaxies.

Gravity The force of attraction that a very large mass, like a planet or a moon, exerts on objects. The pull of the sun's gravity keeps all the planets in orbit.

Hemisphere Earth is split up by the equator into two half spheres, the northern and southern hemispheres.

Lines of latitude Imaginary lines that run around the globe parallel to the equator.

Lines of longitude Imaginary lines that run around the globe from the North to the South Poles. They are used to represent time differences around the world.

Meteors Pieces of rock dust burning up in Earth's atmosphere.

Milky Way The galaxy that Earth is part of. It contains roughly 200 billion stars. We see the Milky Way as a band of stars across the night sky.

Orbiting To circle another object. Earth orbits the sun. The moon orbits Earth.

Planet A ball of rock or gas which orbits a star. There are nine planets in our Solar System.

Pole, North and South The two places on the surface of Earth farthest from the equator.

Seasons The predictable changes in the climate that happen during part of the year. Seasonal change is most obvious in the northern and southern parts of the Earth.

Tropic of Cancer The line of latitude 23° north of the equator. On June 21 the sun is directly overhead the Tropic at noon.

Tropic of Capricorn The line of latitude 23° south of the equator. On December 21 the sun is directly overhead the Tropic at noon.

Waning Getting smaller. The moon wanes as it goes from full moon to new moon.

Waxing Getting bigger. The moon waxes as it goes from new moon to full moon.

Books to read

Asimov, Isaac. *Astronomy Today*. Milwaukee: Gareth Stevens, 1989.

Graham, Ian. *Astronomer*. Be an Expert. New York: Gloucester Press, 1991.

Peacock, Graham. *The Super Science Book of Space*. Super Science. New York: Thomson Learning, 1993.

Schatz, Dennis. *Astronomy Activity Book*. New York: Simon & Schuster Trade, 1991.

Monthly magazines include *Science Scope, Scienceland, Odyssey,* and *Current Science.*

For more information, contact:

NASA, Lyndon B. Johnson Space Center, 2101 NASA Road, Houston, TX 77058

National Air and Space Museum, Smithsonian Institution, Sixth Street & Independence Avenue SW, Washington, DC 20560

Space Camp/Space Academy, The Space & Rocket Center, One Tranquility Base, Huntsville, AL 35807

Chapter notes

Pages 4–5 It is less confusing when describing the rotation of Earth if you always imagine that you are looking down on the North Pole. In that case the instruction counterclockwise is easy to understand. Sundials are not accurate to the minute. Many sophisticated sundials include a table which helps to make them more accurate. The speed of rotation at the surface of Earth decreases the farther north or south you go from the equator. This gives rise to the Coriolis effect which bends weather systems.

Pages 6–7 Make the piece of clay as raised as possible, but make sure it fits under the globe's support. When calculating daylength, try to avoid the periods around the summer and winter solstices as you may get confusing results. Of course, it is impossible to dig through the earth. In fact, no one has even drilled through the relatively thin crust to the mantle layer.

Pages 8–9 The seasons occur because of the tilt of Earth. If it weren't for this tilt there would be no seasons. The tilt of Earth remains constant. It is the effect of moving to the other side of the sun that causes the seasonal effect. Shadows are longer in the winter because the sun is lower in the sky.

Pages 10–11 Pairs of cities that are on the same line of longitude include London in England and Valencia in Spain. Cairns and Sydney in Australia and Miami and Toronto in North America are also good contrasts. On the Arctic and Antarctic circles there is only one day each year when there is 24 hours of daylight. Farther north or south of these lines, respectively, the number is greater.

Pages 12–13 In general, binoculars are a better buy than a telescope. Buy the best you can afford but good results can be obtained from an inexpensive pair. It is most important to find a place well away from streetlights.

Pages 14–15 The moon's volcanoes died out about three billion years ago. Very few rocks of this age are left on Earth's surface because of continued geological and weathering activity. The gravity on the moon's surface is one-sixth that of Earth's surface.

Pages 16–17 The moon orbits Earth counterclockwise. When drawing the phases of the moon, it is important to remember to draw them as seen from Earth. Notice whether the left-hand or the right-hand part of the moon is lit up.

Pages 18–19 It is impossible to devise a practical scale that shows any detail on the planets and also shows them the correct distance apart. When you use a scale showing the sun as a beachball and Jupiter as a pea, Jupiter has to be placed hundreds of yards from the ball. There is a lot of space between the planets!

Pages 20–21 The exact positions of the planets at any time can be found in newspapers and monthly astronomy magazines. If using binoculars, lean against something firm, like a wall or fence, to hold them steady. Galileo was the first to observe the four moons of Jupiter; this led him to understand that everything did not go around Earth as the church of his time taught.

Pages 22–23 The Big Dipper is always visible in the night sky from the northern hemisphere. It can be in different positions around Polaris at different times of year. Since the Big Dipper is part of Ursa Major, astronomers refer to it as an asterism, not a constellation.

Pages 24–25 When going out to observe constellations, leave at least 15 minutes for your eyes to adjust. You will be astonished how much more you can see. Choose an observing site away from any strong lights. The three stars of the Triangle are very bright and obvious. The other stars such as Sagitta are much dimmer. The Milky Way might be difficult to see from a city with streetlights.

Pages 26–27 The Andromeda galaxy is visible with the naked eye, but it is much clearer with binoculars. Constellations are often named after gods and animals from ancient Greek mythology.

Pages 28–29 Meteor trails can be of different colors, ranging from white to yellow and green. Meteor showers usually come from constellations that rise in the eastern sky in early evening. As the constellations move across the sky, the meteors' source will move with them.

Index

Aldebaran 27
Altair 25
Andromeda galaxy 26
Arctic Circle 8, 11
Arcturus 24
axis, Earth's 4, 8, 23

Betelgeuse 27
Big Dipper 22–24
binoculars 12–14
Boötes the Herdsman 24

comets 28
constellations 22–27
craters 14–15
Cygnus the Swan 25

day and night 6–7
daylight 8, 10–13
Deneb 25

Earth 4, 16, 18, 19
equator 9
equinox 11

galaxy 25, 26

Jupiter 18, 19, 21

Leo the Lion 24
light 12–13

lines of latitude 10
lines of longitude 10

Mars 18, 19, 20, 21, 27
Meridian, Greenwich 10
Mercury 19
meteorites 14
meteors 28–29
midnight sun 11
Milky Way galaxy 25–26
moon 13–17

nebula, Orion 27
Neptune 18, 19
night 13
Northern Crown 24
northern hemisphere 8, 11
North Pole 4, 10, 23
North Star 23

Orion the Hunter 27

Pegasus 26
Perseus 26
planets 4, 18–21
Pleiades star cluster 27
Pluto 19
Polaris (North Star) 23

Regulus 24
Rigel 27
rotation, Earth's 4

Sagitta 25
Saturn 18, 19, 21
seasons 4, 7–11
shadowmeter 5
solstice, summer and
   winter 11
Southern Cross 23
South Pole 10
southern hemisphere 23
stars, colors 25
summer 9, 10
sun 4, 12, 18–19
sundials 4–5
sunset and sunrise 7
sun, height 11
sunspots 12

Taurus the Bull 27
telescope 12–13
time 4–6, 10
Triangulum, the Triangle 25

Uranus 19
Ursa Major 23

Vega 25
Venus 18, 19, 20, 21

winter 8, 9, 10

Answers to questions on page 29:
1 True, **2** False, **3** False, **4** True, **5** False, **6** True, **7** False, **8** True